DEAR MOTHER

EKIM

authorHOUSE®

AuthorHouse™
1663 Liberty Drive, Suite 200
Bloomington, IN 47403
www.authorhouse.com
Phone: 1-800-839-8640

First published by AuthorHouse 12/18/2008

Printed in the United States of America
Bloomington, Indiana
This book is printed on acid-free paper.

ISBN: 978-1-4389-2795-4 (sc)
ISBN: 978-1-4389-2796-1 (hc)

CONTENTS

Introduction

CHAPTER ONE   1
The Early Years

CHAPTER TWO   7
Playing Priest

CHAPTER THREE   15
A Kid Growing Up

CHAPTER FOUR   19
Blood is Thicker than Water

CHAPTER FIVE   23
Holidays

CHAPTER SIX   29
High School Days

CHAPTER SEVEN   35
My Work Life

CHAPTER EIGHT   39
Bus Driving Days

CHAPTER NINE   45
Moving On

CHAPTER TEN   47
My "Hard Hat" Days

CHAPTER ELEVEN   51
Mom's Last Days

CHAPTER TWELVE   57
Change in Management

CHAPTER THIRTEEN   63
  Dad

CHAPTER FOURTEEN   67
  Shriners Hospital for Children

CHAPTER FIFTEEN   71
  The Theatre

CHAPTER SIXTEEN   75
  My "Other" Love

CHAPTER SEVENTEEN   89
  What It All Means
  Epilogue

INTRODUCTION

THROUGHOUT EVERYONE'S LIFE, SITUATIONS OCCUR every day that make us stop and think about what just happened. Some are quite funny while others are very sad. The main idea is that what was funny to me may not have been funny to anyone else. When I introduced this book to my friends, I received positive response about its content. As a matter of fact, I saw the reactions that I was looking for. As I wrote this book, I was reminded about a lot of things from my childhood and what I had done as a teenager growing up in the sixties. Most of my friends who are almost my age could associate with what had happened to me as a boy growing up in a small town. If this book does nothing else, I hope it will bring a smile to your face and possibly a tear to your eye as you let your mind go back to that time of innocence.

Chapter One

THE EARLY YEARS

Snuggled deep inside the covers with only my nose exposed to the elements in the bedroom, I was enveloped in four inches of bedding materials. I had the bottom bunk, and my brother, sound asleep, took refuge on the top. Our room was big enough for the bunk bed, a four-drawer dresser, and a metal two-door closet to the right of the window. The ice covered the window on the inside, since there was no direct heat in our room. The floor vent, which allowed the heat to escape to the second level of the duplex, was open, but the air flow took all of the warmth to mom and dad's room in the front of the house.

I would lean over to the window, and with my fingernail, expose my sleepy eyes to the outside by scratching away the ice just enough so I could see the old foundry just past the backyard. Nothing was moving outside because it was a deep, frozen, cold morning. All I wanted to do was keep the warmth that had generated under the covers right where it was. I knew in just a few seconds dad would be saying, "You boys get up". It's a school day." My brother and I reacted very quickly when dad spoke those words unlike the extra time that was taken when mom called us. We knew there was no "rest for the wicked" when dad barked his orders.

Being closest to the floor in the lower bunk, I was up and dressed first. The main reason was that the bathroom was only made for one unless you got trapped on the pot by someone brushing their teeth or washing the night's sleep out of their eyes. Also, the quicker you could get dressed and out of the bathroom, the quicker you could go downstairs, and be welcomed by the fresh perked coffee, mom's cinnamon toast, and heat from the warm stove in the front room. Dad was always the last one down, and he would see to it that the floor vent was closed shut so the warmth would stay downstairs. Mom spent a great deal of her day ironing in the kitchen on the Maytag roller ironer. It was the one where you would sit with your leg under the roller and use your knee to activate it. She would allow me to do handkerchiefs only if I had to stay home due to illness, or when it was the weekend.

The kitchen was the main room on our side of the duplex. "Sarge," my grandmother, lived on the other side. We called her Sarge because she watched us kids when my mom and dad weren't home. She was fair but firm. Thus, the name Sarge seemed to fit then, and it did our whole life.

Getting ready for school was not so difficult. Attending the Catholic school made it really easy to decide what clothes would be worn today. It was always the same—blue pants, white shirt, and blue tie for us boys, and for the girls, a blue skirt, and white blouse with these wide blue straps that came up over the shoulder and down the front attaching to the front of the skirt. The boys always assumed it was so designed to mask the female growth spurt that seemed to happen between the fifth and the ninth grades. The girls would fidget with the extra material in such a way that it would allow us boys to just imagine what the real reason for the extra material was. We patiently waited for the spring season so there would be less uniform and more flesh to see. Little did we know that they had it well under control. My brother and I would ride with my dad, since his office was in the same direction as the school. On those cold days, there was no garage to keep the car warm. We would run from the house to the car, and as dad opened the car door locks, we would pile into the front seat and get as close to the car heater as possible. The humidity would begin to rise inside the car, and the windows began to look like our bedroom windows—covered with ice. The car defroster, whining at the very beginning of its heat-up phase, would not put out any heat until we were arriving at the school. My dad would instruct us to pull off our gloves and place our bare hands on the freezing front windows to melt the ice. This would allow him to see so he could drive. My brother and I made it a competition to see who could keep his hands on the window the longest. The first one who pulled his hand away was the loser. I was always the winner because my brother would pull his hands away. I didn't realize until later that all he was doing was using me to follow my dad's orders. By pulling his hands away, he kept warm while I sat there keeping the window clear with my numb hands. He was always smarter than I was.

The walk to the school building was well orchestrated by the nuns as well as the movement inside. For the longest time, I really thought that boys and girls were never made to be together. "Boys to the right and girls to the left." Those were the everyday orders. We became so used to this that it became a way of life, at least inside the school walls. We learned at an early age that standing in the hallway at certain times, and at very strategic locations, would allow us to peer into the girls' bathroom so that just every once in awhile we could get a glimpse of those wide pieces of material affixed to the front of the uniform dress in some precarious positions that allowed our wonderment to be cured. We learned not to get caught by the principal, Sister Mary Martin, or we would find ourselves kneeling in front of her office with a "glow in the dark" rosary in hand for a minimum of one hour. This was the ultimate humiliation and a very effective punishment for trying to get a "quick peek." My knees would hurt for days.

The school consisted of grades one through twelve, and unlike today, there was a nun for every class. The living quarters were adjacent to the school, which allowed the school to remain open even in the worst weather conditions. We had no such thing as a snow day. However, we did have our famous " First Fridays," which allowed us time off from the regular studies but not the

4

required attendance at mass. (First Friday was a special day when the entire school would go to Mass and then eat breakfast before starting classes) We were always asked, "How many will be staying for breakfast after mass tomorrow, and how many doughnuts would you like?" The bakery was less than a half block away and provided the school with fresh glazed doughnuts that were the size of a bread plate. When I was asked for my breakfast order, I always held up both hands and all fingers just to confuse the counter. I always seemed to get only two, no matter how many I ordered.

Chapter Two

PLAYING PRIEST

ANOTHER PREPARATION FOR THE FIRST Friday was when all the students in school went to confession in the church on Thursday, the day before the First Friday. The senior class was commanded by the principal to walk to the church, "boys to the right and girls to the left," to tell their sins so they could receive Holy Communion the next day. We had three priests in the parish and all three would hear the students' confessions. Two regular confessionals and one temporary foldout confessional were used when the entire school had to go to confess. A senior boy was always asked to go to the church and get the temporary foldout confessional ready for the pastor to use. The old pastor always used the foldout because it allowed him to come and go as he pleased. He had some problems that required him to leave the foldout every once in awhile. We boys would bet each other as to the type of problems that he had. These would range from bladder problems, to intestinal problems, to drinking problems, and everything in between. The priests lived right next to the church so it was very easy for them to come and go, and they did.

My turn came to set up the foldout confessional and I took advantage of the situation. I was sent to the church to get the apparatus out of the closet and get it set up before the senior class got to the church. I went to the back room where I found the confessional, and I took it to its regular location in the side aisle facing the altar. While I was finishing the final touches to the foldout, the senior class came into the church following their "boys to the right and girls to the left" command. Then they sat in their assigned pews. It just so happened that the location of the foldout confessional that I so carefully had set up was on the left side. The old pastor had not made it to the church from the rectory but the girls didn't know that. All they could see was someone in the foldout confessional. They assumed it was the old pastor and that he was open for business. However, it wasn't the old pastor; it was me! What was I to do? Should I leave and miss the opportunity of a lifetime for a young boy, or should I stay and play priest? I knew all of the words to say to someone who was about to confess their sins. My voice was deep enough to sound the part. I peeked around the partition to see who was first and saw it was Anne Marie. This piqued my curious mind, because I knew that she had some really good sins to report.

With a tissue paper folded neatly on her head, and with her hands folded in prayer, Anne Marie headed to her confessional thinking the old pastor was there to listen and forgive. However, in reality, I was there strictly to hear what she had done. What power this would give me in my circle of friends. I would be the coolest of the cool.

"In the name of the Father and of the Son and of the Holy Ghost, Amen," I said.

Anne Marie began, "Bless me, Father, for I have sinned. It has been one month since my last confession."

My mind now began to race as I tried to imagine what she was about to tell me. She was "one of those girls" that the guys knew about. She always had a boyfriend from the public school, and we all knew what that meant. She was about to tell me.

"I ate meat on Friday, said a bad word to myself about Sarah, and had some impure thoughts about my boyfriend."

Then there was silence. I am thinking, "Is that it? Ate meat on Friday, said a bad word to herself, and had an impure thought about her boyfriend?" That was the extent of her sins for this month? You have got to be kidding me.

Just as I was about to ask her if she was sure that was all, I heard the door to the side entrance to the church open and close. As I turned to see what it was, all I could see was the old pastor coming down the hall heading to the foldout confessional. I immediately stood up, got behind the curtain that was draped on the back of the wooden frame, and crept out the back so I would not be seen. Ann Marie was still waiting for a response to her sins. When the old pastor got into place, he asked her to begin. The look on her face was priceless, but I was really let down that she didn't have more to confess. For the rest of the year, I always wondered what else she had to say. I always wanted to ask her, but I couldn't figure out a way to tell her that it was me listening to her confession. I just knew if the old pastor ever found out, I would be in deep, deep trouble, and I would go straight to hell when I died.

I did play priest one other time. However, I never had the opportunity to hear confessions again. I did, however, have the opportunity to buy beer while clothed as a priest sporting a black suit with a Roman collar, all which made me look very authentic.

During my senior year, we played in the state Catholic basketball tournament, and during the course of the games, we were housed in the hotel next to the sports stadium. Two senior boys were assigned to a room, and adults were also assigned to various rooms on the same floor as the team. The room next to ours was occupied by one of the assistant priests so we were kept well under control. A group of us was in our room playing cards, and the adults were attending a "special meeting" in the hotel. As a result, we were left on our own and told to stay in our rooms. After a couple dozen games of cards, it was suggested that we find a Coke machine in the hall and get something to drink. It was then the suggestion was made by yours truly that we should go find some beer and bring it back to the room. "How can we do that?" was the big question. I had already thought about the problem before I made the suggestion that we go find some beer. The priest next door was my size, and I knew that he had brought a change of clothes with him. So I told the guys that were there to stay put and I would be right back. We had adjoining rooms, and the door between our room and the priest's room was unlocked so he could keep an eye on us. I opened the door and found his black suit with his Roman collar neatly folded on the bed. I slipped out of my clothes, put on the suit, and buttoned the collar in place. I had black shoes for our morning attendance at church, and they made the uniform complete. I went out the front door and knocked on my bedroom door.

When Chuck, my teammate, answered the door, his only response was, "You are going straight to hell."

After a good laugh by everyone, and a collection was taken, I stuffed the money into my pocket, and out the door I went to buy beer.

We were on the eighth floor of the hotel so I decided to take the elevator to the lobby, where I knew there was a shop that sold beer, pop and snacks. I pushed the down button and waited for the car to climb to the eighth floor. When the door opened, to my surprise, there were three ladies in the car heading also to the lobby.

I stepped into the car and was met with, "Good *evening, Father.*"

I acknowledged with a resounding, *"Good evening,"* and kept looking straight ahead.

I counted to myself as we passed each floor until the bell in the elevator sounded our location. It seemed like it had taken ten minutes for the elevator to reach the lobby, but when it did, and the doors opened, I looked back at the ladies and said, "*You ladies have a good evening.*"

They responded, "*You, too, Father.*"

Lucky for me the snack shop was right across from the elevator, so I headed straight into it after the ladies started into the center lobby. I never missed a beat; went straight to the cooler, picked up two six-packs of Iron City, and headed to the counter to pay for my beverages. Now mind you, I was eighteen years old, dressed up like a priest, and looked like I was twenty-six, with two six-packs in my hands.

The woman behind the counter looked at me and said, "It looks like you're going to a party, Father."

I smiled and said, "Something like that, bless you."

She handed me the change, and I was off to get back to the eighth floor as quickly as I could. My timing was perfect, or my guardian angel was working overtime, because the door to the elevator was open. As I went inside, I pushed the number eight button about a dozen times. The doors closed with no one else aboard. Before I knew it, I was standing in my hallway. Timing was again on my side, because the meeting for the adults was not over yet, and the hallway was clear. I knocked on my hotel room door, and it was obvious that my teammates not only thought I was crazy, but knew I was crazy. They couldn't believe I had pulled it off. We drank the twelve beers and made it to bed prior to the adults returning for bed check. We good Catholic boys would never get ourselves into trouble, and oh, by the way, we won the state tournament the next day.

One of the guys took a picture of me in my priestly garb, and I only showed it to my mom about four years later.

Her comment was, "What would you have done if you had run into the bishop in the hallway?"

I told her that I would have kissed his ring and run like hell. If the truth be known, I never really thought about it. At eighteen years old, I had no fear.

Chapter Three

A KID GROWING UP

GROWING UP ON VIRGINIA AVENUE was an adventure. You have to picture duplex wooden frame houses situated so close together that we could walk between them and touch both houses at the same time. Needless to say, we were very close to our neighbors. There were no secrets on our block. Everyone knew everyone's business. The street was our playground most of the time. Traffic was not an issue on "Bed Bug Row" as it was affectionately called. We had a store on the corner that sold milk and bread, but it mainly sold beer. Therefore, we kids were not allowed to go there unless mom sent us for some bread. I remember going after bread, which cost eleven cents. I would get fifteen cents, and the four cents in change went into the Spanish peanut container that sat on the bar. I would have to sit on the stool so I could reach the big glass bowl and the slot where my four pennies would go. I can remember growing bigger so I wouldn't have to sit on the stool. By then, I was still getting the Spanish peanuts, but I would also get a dime Coke and drop the peanuts in the Coke. Then I could drink and eat the peanuts at the same time.

The Corner Store, as it was called, also served as a backstop for our three-man rubber ball game. We would have a batter standing with his back to the brick building, and across the street one would be the pitcher, and the other would be the umpire. The trick was to throw as hard as you could and strike out the batter. If the ball was hit, the umpire would then determine, depending on how hard it was hit, how many bases you would get. Many a night, after a nine-inning game, we would go home covered with welts left by the rubber ball that found its target on our backs, legs, or shoulders. It was an unwritten rule of the street that you would never intentionally try to hit the batter. However, if you got hit with the ball, you always remembered your turn to pitch was coming up.

Another game that was part of the growing-up process was bicycle tag. This was for all ages, except the real little ones, and was played every night before dark. This game tested your agility both as a bicycle rider and a runner. The playing court was set up usually in the intersection of the streets. The game consisted of four people on bikes, and the rest—as many as wanted to play— trying not to be touched by one of the bike riders. The bike riders could not take their feet off the pedals, and once they touched you, you had to sit down, and stay off the court until another member of your team would come and touch you (save you). Then you could continue to play. As a runner, you would try to get the bike riders to run into each other, causing them to have to sit out if their feet touched the ground. Once your team was all sitting down, the game was over, and you would start over with different bikers and different runners. It really didn't take much to keep us busy while we were growing up.

Summer brought the opening of the county playground on "Bed Bug Row." This was the "nickname" of our street. Organized games, competition, hot dog roasts, volleyball games, and sometimes good-looking playground instructors, were the orders for the day. As boys trying to prepare for the ways of the world, we always were interested in who was going to be the instructor this year. The county would select its instructors from applicants who were seniors in high school or those who had just graduated. We were just young Catholic boys ready to learn whatever the instructor wanted to teach. No doubt there were times when we learned some things that were not part of the county playground instructor guidelines.

The instructors that were hired by the county were always female, and that was a good thing for us guys. Short shorts and county playground T-shirts were the common dress for the job. Now, in the six years that I attended the playground activities, during five of the six years, we had the cream of the crop when it came to good-looking instructors, or at least us guys thought so. Let's face it, that was the big draw to get to the playground the first thing in the morning. From my bedroom, I could look out my back window, watch for her car to come down the street, and make the right turn into the alley, which led up the hill to the playground. I had it timed that as soon as she rounded the corner, I would be down the stairs, out the front door, up the sidewalk, between the sixth and seventh house, through their backyard, and be standing at the storage shed as she pulled up in her 1955 Ford convertible. Early on, I would refer to her as "teacher" or "Miss Brown." But as the weeks went on, and we became more comfortable with each other, she became "Kathy." Eight years difference in age didn't make any difference in my head, and it wasn't until she was visited by her "boyfriend," Ted, that I realized that I was living in another world. Quickly, the excitement of the whole experience came to an end. I didn't visit the playground that often anymore, and one day when I saw her coming down the alley, she stopped and asked me where I had been. She hadn't seen me for some time. I told her that my dog had been sick, and I had to take care of him.

As she spun her tires, she yelled, "I hope he gets better," and off she went; probably to see Ted.

That ended my playground scene, and as a soon-to-be ten-year-old, I had to move on to other things in life.

Chapter Four

BLOOD IS THICKER THAN WATER

I LOVED SPORTS AND WAS willing to play any sport, at any time, with anyone. Basketball was my favorite. I was blessed with some height for a boy of my age, and thus it was easy to pick me out in the school pictures. Being taller and huskier than most kids my age, I usually got picked first for a team. My brother, on the other hand, was usually last because of his size. On one particular afternoon, he and I went to the neighborhood schoolyard to play horse. We had been playing for about fifteen minutes when we were approached by this bigger kid from another neighborhood. I was shooting the ball, and my brother was getting the rebound when this kid grabbed the ball from him. He said it was his ball, and he was taking it home. My brother protested vocally, and he found himself being pushed to the ground. Now this really made me mad. Not only did he push my brother to the ground, but he was taking our basketball.

"Hey!" I yelled to him. "What the hell do you think you're doing?"

"I'm taking my ball home," he growled.

"I don't think so," I said, and went after him with my fist drawn back and moving full throttle ahead. I had every intention of getting our ball back any way I could. I was running so fast, and throwing a punch from way down south at the same time, that I failed to see his right fist coming straight at my face. I remember sitting up and seeing my brother standing over me.

He said, "What did you think you were going to do? When you were swinging at him, you were ten feet away. You tripped, fell forward, and he caught you with one punch."

I shook my head and looked around. Heading up over the hill was the boy from the other neighborhood. Laying on the foul line was our basketball. My brother and I brushed ourselves off, picked up our ball, and headed for home. We never told a soul about our game of horse on that day.

My brother and I had the complete "run" of the house—as much as my dad would allow us—until the big event occurred—the birth of my sister. When she arrived on this earth, the freedom that my brother and I had felt for all those years was suddenly cast into the depths of the sea. She became the ruler of the universe. We couldn't do anything unless she was involved. And she got involved in everything. She was put on the earth for only one reason—to torment my brother and me. If we were playing ball, she had to play. If we were riding our stick horses, she had to ride along with us. If we were throwing crab apples at the windows in the factory behind us, then she was throwing crab apples also. Thus, having to be associated in every aspect of our lives, it's no wonder she was such a "tomboy." All the boys of her age were afraid of her. She could throw harder and farther than they could. She could ride her bike faster than they could, and yes, she could kick their butts whenever she wanted. I signed up for judo class one time, and my mom said that she wanted my sister to take the lessons also. So, every Tuesday and Thursday, we both went to judo class. By the time it was all over, she had her brown belt at age ten, and she could throw any man, of any size, at any time. Believe me, I know. Somehow, all those early days of having to include my sister, as much as we did as we were growing up, allowed us to be that much closer. My mom must have known what she was doing.

Chapter Five

HOLIDAYS

HOLIDAYS WERE ALWAYS A BIG thing for my family. The neighborhood was laid out such that my grandma, Sarge, lived on the other side of the duplex from us, and my other grandma and grandpa lived about five houses up on the next street. So, when it was time to celebrate something like a birthday, or a First Communion, it was easy to get the family together. Sarge had the biggest dining room and the largest table where everyone would sit. If there were others invited, the old faithful card table would be set up, and we kids would know our place. So, it was quite an honor to be able to sit with the adults at the "big" table at times. All the cooking was accomplished in Grandma Sarge's kitchen, a very small 10'x10' area that had a small four-burner stove with a fairly large oven. There was one small table that had two chairs that were removed and utilized at the dining room table. This also gave the two cooks, my mom and Sarge, room enough to create their most delicious feasts. When the family all got together, we never wanted for food. Although many times during the week when there was no "big dinner," we were given what we were to eat, and that was it. My dad would announce to us boys that "the kitchen was closed," and we knew that was it. Snacking was not part of our vocabulary. The reason for the tight controls by my dad was that he was not making a lot of money. Actually no one was during those days. He was an insurance man and spent most of his time traveling from house to house collecting his accounts. Those were the days when the insurance agents actually came to your house and collected your insurance premiums. At the end of the month, each of the agents would have to call their accounts and check their account books for the amount of money that they collected during the month. It had to balance with their books. During that period of the month, we would have to walk very quietly, and not make any noise, so we didn't disrupt my dad's accounting process. I can still hear his old-time adding machine clicking and clicking as he kept trying to make column A balance with column B. All month long, he would have access to the company's money as he collected his accounts. In most cases, he would have to make change for his clients. The bad part was that things were so tight he would occasionally have to "borrow" from the company to pay a bill and then try to make it up by the end of the month. Sometimes he came up short, and we would all have to pay for it by being "extra good" as my mom used to say. Eventually, my mom went to work and it made things a little easier.

The first six grades of Catholic school were fairly well regimented with religion, English, Latin, science and French. If it wasn't for basketball, life would have been dull. Competition among the schools started in the fourth grade and lasted until I graduated. It was during those formidable years that the parish priests tried to convince me that I should go to the preparatory seminary to study for the priesthood. As a "little guy," during the evening, as our family would sit around the living room of my grandmother's house saying the rosary, the evening would always end with me "saying Mass" for everyone. My mom would sit back proudly as I rattled off the Latin prayers that were said daily at a real Mass. I was an altar boy, and I served Mass whenever I could.

I thought it was cool to be dressed in the cassock and surplus praying along with the priest. It also gave me the opportunity to place the communion patton under the chin of all receiving communion, especially the girls. (The patton was a gold plate that was placed under the chin of the person receiving communion so as to catch any small pieces of the wafer that the priest placed on the person's tongue) Just to make an impression, I would always give the cute ones a little bump on the neck as my secret way of saying hello. Usually, it caused them some confusion, because they would forget to stick out their tongue, and the priest would have to remind them. I would just stand there and smile. My mom would have really been happy if I had become a priest, but it wasn't in the cards.

Chapter Six

HIGH SCHOOL DAYS

MY HIGH SCHOOL DAYS WERE really cool. My brother and I started a rock and roll band and we actually played for other school dances. There was nothing better than being in a band and playing at a public school dance. I would sing and play steel guitar. My brother was the drummer, and we had two other guitar players. Rock and roll was so easy to play. As long as you knew the three cords, "C," "F" and "G," you could play almost any song, and the girls thought we were really something else. I was in the eighth grade when I finally realized why I wasn't going to the seminary. It was at that time when I discovered cheerleaders, majorettes, and short shorts. *"Dear Mother"* *(This was an expression that my mom always used when she didn't know what to say).* It was quite a dilemma trying to keep the Catholic girls happy, while at the same time doing everything I could to get to the other school where the majorettes always practiced on the football field.

There was something about those other girls at the public school. They always seemed to be more flirtatious especially with us Catholic boys. It was probably the short shorts that they always wore and the noted T-shirts that made us constantly stare at them. We never realized what we were doing but it sure did look mighty fine. One girl had especially caught my eye. Her name was Carrie Lee. She was a small-framed girl who really could fill out a majorette uniform. White knee-high boots and short shorts accentuated her figure, and she had the personality to match. I got up my courage, one day after their practice, to go over and talk with her. It was all downhill after that. She didn't have a steady boyfriend, and her dad owned a local car dealership. That's why she always drove a new car. What else could I ever want? She was a high school majorette, drove a new car, and had a personality to match. We dated a couple of times, went to the show, and a couple of dances. The date I really remember was when we drove to the city park to ride around in her new sports car. I was driving. We were laughing and having a good time. I was paying more attention to her than to the road when all of a sudden we came upon an exit that was closed. It had a steel bar that stretched across the road and sat at the height of the front windshield. As I pulled her down on the seat, I saw the bar coming right at the windshield. I jammed on the brakes, and the car slid straight into the steel bar. We stopped with only inches to spare. It scared us so badly that we hardly said another thing as we drove home. The next time I saw her she was walking with a good friend of mine. I remember saying to myself, "Well, there goes the new car." The two of them got married and stayed together for a number of years. He represented me during my first divorce. Isn't it interesting how those things work out?

I bought my first car when I was sixteen years old. I paid $50.00 for a 1950 Crosley that had been setting out in the field for about five years. Flat tires, bees, and broken glass were the order of the day. I think my dad was just as excited as I was when I asked him to go look at it with me. He used to work for Ford Motor Company as head of the parts department, so he knew a lot about fixing up cars. When we went across town to see the car, he told me all the things that would have to be done to it before it would be street worthy. When we got to the location, the gentleman who owned the car gave us the keys. We went out to the back lot, and there it was, with its dry rot tires and all. I opened the driver's door and had to swat the wasps from my head because the inside of the car was loaded with them. My dad had some bug spray in his car so we fumigated the inside of the car, and I was finally able to climb behind the wheel. The owner of the car said the motor would run and that we could drive it up the alley to try it out. I put in the key and turned it to what I thought should start it up, but nothing happened. I looked at the dashboard, and then realized that there was a button to push to start the engine. I hit the button and to our amazement it started. To me, it sounded like a well-tuned race car. To my dad, all he could say was, "It needs some work." I paid the owner the $50.00

and climbed back into the car for my initial journey home. My dad followed me in his car, since I didn't have any license plates. All was going well until I hit a straight stretch of road about a mile from the house. All of a sudden I heard this sound like metal dragging on the concrete. I stopped and my dad was already out of the car and looking underneath. He announced that the flywheel had broken loose from the transmission and that would have to be the first thing we fixed. We were about a block away from the repair shop, so I walked to the shop, and had them come and tow my new purchase into the repair bay. They told me it would be about a week before they could get to it, and they would call me when it was ready. The cost would be about $75.00. I didn't have any choice. That was the longest week in my life. (*My dad knew the owner of the repair shop so it really didn't cost me $75.00. They only charged me $20.00.*)

The call came through and my car was ready. I walked to the repair shop and drove my car to its new home—my backyard. My dad and I spent many hours working on the car to get it street ready. We added new hoses, spark plugs, oil filter, distributor, fan belts, gaskets, and an exhaust system, to name a few of the items that I can remember. The engine was so small that we took off the motor mounts, and we lifted the engine out of the car by hand. This was really the first time that my dad and I did something together besides cat fishing. We painted the engine well black, and the engine itself we painted bright red. It really looked cool when we got it all back together; even down to the interior carpet. I got a large carpet piece from a church that was changing its interior carpet to tile. There was enough to cover the interior of the doors, floors, and headliner of the car. It was really a sight to behold. The car lasted for six months until one day when I was parking it in front of my house. I would always come down the street and make a U-turn in front of my house and park facing the opposite way. This day, as I turned the wheel to make my U-turn, I heard a crack, and the right side of the car dropped about four inches. When I got out of the car to inspect it, I saw that the main leaf spring had broken. If I couldn't find a replacement spring, the Crosley was history. As my life would have it, there was no replacement spring anywhere in the area, so I nursed the car to the closest garage. Then I became the proud owner of a 1958 used Fiat. Total cost with trade-in was $100.00. There were always problems with the car. It spent more time in the shop than on the road. By the way, the car dealership was owned by the dad of the majorette that I had dated earlier. So, I got up my nerve and went to see him about my car. He sympathized with me, and I walked out of his office with a much newer 1960 Fiat that ran very well. I was so proud of myself. So was my dad. I guess dating his daughter didn't hurt me. God help me if he ever found out that we almost killed ourselves in one of his cars.

My senior year was, without a doubt, one of the greatest years of my life. I was very successful in sports and survived the classroom under the rule of the good sisters of Saint Joseph. Of course, the only two sports offered at the school were basketball and baseball. I think the real reason was that I didn't want to shame my mom, and I was scared to death of my dad. So if you combine all of those forces, I really had to be successful in school.

As senior boys, we were often called upon to assist with the cleaning of the two fire escapes that were on opposite sides of the school. One of the "tubes," as they were called, serviced the high school wing of the building, while the other "tube" serviced the junior high and elementary side of the building. The school was four stories tall, so when you went down the tubes, it was very close to the sensation you get on a waterslide except there was no water. The day prior to the school having a fire drill, the principal would call upon six senior boys to wear potato sacks. Our job was to slide down the fire escape a number of times for the sole purpose of cleaning out the pigeon poop from the inside of the tube. The birds set up residence early in the year and fire prevention month was October. So, during the last week of September, we would be cleaning out the slide. What we found out was that the more we would go down the tube, the more slippery it became. We would really work on the high school side because the girls would go down really fast. It was the job of the physical education teacher to stand at the bottom and catch the students as they were spit out of the tube. Of course, the girls would come out not always sitting upright, and those uniforms would sometimes get all dislodged. All I remember is that on the days we had fire drills, the P.E. teacher always seemed really happy.

Chapter Seven

MY WORK LIFE

I WANTED TO GO TO college and become a teacher. I felt with all of the wrong things that I did, I could prepare kids for life by explaining what not to do. At least that was my plan. The state college that was in my hometown was very inexpensive. I could take fourteen hours per semester, and it would only cost me $200.00. So there was no real pressure to earn enough money to go on to school. Four hundred dollars per year was not bad at all. During my first summer out of high school, I worked in this large glass plant on the other side of town. My Fiat was still running (*I can still see that steel bar coming right at my face),* so I had transportation to the plant. I was hired to work on the tipple, which was a very high railroad track that ran above large round bins filled with different colors of broken glass. My job was to walk alongside the box cars that were slowly moving on the track. With a sledge hammer, I beat on the sides of the cars to loosen the wet, colored glass that came in the car, and it would then fall into the bins. This glass would come from other factories as wasted glass, and we would melt it down and reuse it in some other glass product. This was recycling in 1964. The job paid $5.50 per hour, which wasn't bad for an eighteen-year-old kid wanting to go to college. By the end of summer, I had made my tuition money and could cover my car payment for the rest of the year. The union at the plant allowed part-time help to work for sixty-two days, and then we would be let go. This meant that I would have to find another job that would allow me to go to school and work at the same time. The perfect job was offered to me by a friend who worked as a pharmacist in a local drugstore. They were looking for someone who could deliver prescriptions, stock shelves, and keep the store clean. I was their man. For four years, I worked for the drugstore and still found time to study and graduate.

My college days seemed to fly by. With the war always looking over my shoulder, I tried to keep as busy as possible. Oh, yes, there were frat parties, sports, and more frat parties. I was president of the fraternity for two years. Nobody was president for two years in a row, but I had to straighten the group out. They had been on social probation for two years before I joined, and I was bound and determined to get them back in good standing with the administration. It seems that one evening a group of

36

the members broke into the athletic department and stole the 16mm projector. They then took it to a local establishment for a special viewing of some questionable films. The party was raided by the local police and all materials and equipment, including the athletic department projector, were confiscated. This is what caused the social probation and reputation. I had my job cut out for me. However, after two years, we were back in good graces, and I figured it was time to leave the fraternity on a positive note. I became an inactive member, because I had a full-time job and too many conflicts in my schedule. If the truth be known, I just wanted to get out and away from the foolishness.

I dated a girl throughout high school and college. We made plans many times about getting married and raising a family in our hometown. This is what Catholic kids do in small towns. Your family, friends and the entire community that knows you expect it. So we did. We got married in June of 1968, and by March of 1969, our first child was born. This is what Catholic kids do from small towns.

The teaching degree that I had earned allowed my wife and me to move near Washington D.C., since their counties were paying the most for new teachers. My annual salary was $5,800.00. (*Dear Mother*) Now, with a wife and child and another one on the way (*Catholic kids are expected to do this*), I had to once again find additional work, and I did.

One day at lunch one of my students asked me what school teachers did in the summertime for work. At that time I had planned to erect outdoor metal sheds. (*Bah*) He said that his dad had said that the bus company he worked for wanted to hire some teachers to act as tour conductors and part-time bus drivers for the summer. So, I made a call and the next thing I knew I was rolling down the capitol beltway in a fifty-two-foot-long bus. *(Ralph Kramden, eat your heart out.)* While I was in college, I had worked some weekends for UPS washing the tractors while the trailers were being unloaded. I had learned to drive tractor-trailer rigs then, so driving the bus was a "piece of cake." This was a good job except for the fact that we were put on what the company called vacation tours, which caused me to go out of town a great deal. I did see a lot of the country, but I missed seeing my family, which now was two daughters, my wife, and another one on the way. *(Dear Mother)*

Chapter Eight

Bus Driving Days

THE BUS DRIVING JOB WAS not without incident. On one particular tour through upstate New York, two of my forty-six passengers were nuns. They happened to be sitting on the right side of the bus in the front elevated seats. We were on our way to dinner in this small New York town. I was trying to make up some time, because the group had delayed our departure from a cathedral, and we were going to be late for dinner. I was going a little faster than I should have, and as I came around a turn, there was a local police car with radar attached. As I passed the police car, I kept looking out the side mirrors of the bus, and I finally saw the lights on the roof of the police car light up. My quick thinking made me turn to the two nuns in the front seat. I asked them, in about two minutes, would they mind walking to the back of the bus and look out the back window and wave. They agreed to my request. By now, I was stopped on the side of the road, and the police car was sitting behind me. I quickly grabbed my log book, opened the door, and proceeded back to the police car. I met the officer at the rear of the bus. I was in the process of explaining to him that I was carrying a group of nuns, we were on our way to attend Mass in town, and we were running a little late. At that precise moment, the two nuns from inside the bus peeked out the back window and waved to the policeman. He tipped his hat and told me that he would escort us to the town line in hopes that we wouldn't have to be late. When I got back into the bus, the sisters asked me if they had done all right. I told them they had done just right, and away we went down the road with no ticket and a police escort. (*Dear Mother*)

ﻉ ﻉ ﻉ

THEN THERE WAS THE TIME I drove for the Clowns of America to their annual meeting in Philadelphia. They were a great group of people from all walks of life who belonged to a troupe in Baltimore. Every year they traveled to Philadelphia to meet with other troupes from around the country and "clown around." (*No pun intended.*) I always tried to have fun with the passengers and this group made it very easy. We sang, told jokes, and had talent shows while traveling up the turnpike. When we returned to Baltimore and the trip was over, they asked me if they could request me for next year's trip. I said, "Of course," but under one condition—I would be allowed to dress in a complete clown outfit. The next year came around and sure enough, I was requested to drive for the same group. I was not surprised that when I pulled up in front of their pickup location, that they handed me a clown outfit complete with a red hairpiece and a big red, round nose. I went in a restroom, took off my bus uniform, and put on the outfit. You should have heard the ovation when I came out of the restroom. I drove all the way as "Billy the Clown" and greeted three different toll officers with the biggest smile and a honk of my horn on the turnpike. I had a ball, and at the end of the trip, the group presented me with an honorary clown certificate. It was by far the best trip I ever had.

❧ ❧ ❧

THEN THERE WAS THE TIME that I drove Colt Corral #75 to the enshrinement of Gino Marchetti into the Pro Football Hall of Fame in Canton, Ohio. I picked up the group at a bar on the West side of Baltimore at 6:00 p.m. The trip to Canton would take about eight hours. As I stood beside the bus waiting for everyone to board, I noticed the amount of beer that was being loaded and the trays of subs being carried onto the bus. They brought enough on board to feed the entire crowd at the football game for two days. The leader of the group paid the bill before we left. As he put it, he probably wouldn't be awake when we returned the next evening. We pulled away from the curb about 6:30 p.m. and started west. There was singing and joking going on and lots of drinking. Six hours later and with no rest stops, we were coming out of Pennsylvania, which is somewhat mountainous at that location. I noticed the group leader coming toward me from the back of the bus. It was dark by now so I couldn't see much in the back of the bus.

The group leader tapped me on the shoulder and said, "Mike, you are a hell of a driver. You amazed me how you were able to drive this bus down those mountains, but I have one question for you. What kind of plumber are you?"

I said, "Plumber? What are you talking about?"

He then told me that the toilet was overflowing, and the contents were running down the aisle.

I turned on some of the inside lights and realized he was telling the truth. We normally tried to stop every two to three hours and have the passengers "stretch" for a couple of minutes. However, this group said there was a bathroom on board, and they wanted to get there, so they didn't want to stop. They had consumed so much beer and utilized the facility so much that it was more than full. Now what do I do? We are now on the Ohio Turnpike and it is about 1:00 a.m. Yes, I did come up with a plan. I told the group leader to go back to the bathroom and locate a lever that was on the backside of the toilet. Then, when he saw the lights blink inside the toilet room, he was to lift the lever. I watched him stagger back to the toilet and go inside the room. As he disappeared, I looked out to my left and right mirrors and straight ahead into the darkness. The Ohio Turnpike at this point was very straight, so I turned off my headlights and running lights which allowed me to see there were no cars anywhere near us. I then flipped the switch which controlled the lights in the restroom. I glanced at my right-hand mirror only to witness the baptism of the Ohio Turnpike. Streaming behind the bus was a vapor trail of toilet water and tissue paper for about a quarter of a mile. The ovation that came from the passengers was not as great as the Clowns of America, but they certainly appreciated the fact that "Mike, besides being a hell of a driver," was in fact also a "plumber." No more water was running down the aisle. I got the group to their motel at 2:00 a.m., and I spent the next three hours cleaning and mopping out the bus. *(Dear Mother)*

Chapter Nine

Moving On

I HAVE MANY MORE BUS stories like the ones I just described, and they are all true. My bus driver days lasted four years, and my family now included my wife, my two daughters, and my son. I really needed to be home.

Three kids in diapers, a three-bedroom slab on grade rancher, and one bathroom didn't allow for much room. We had lines stretched all over the house from wall to wall. There was no such thing as diaper service. The process was simple—dump it into the toilet and let it soak in the tub. It's amazing how you can make things work.

The good Lord always looks out for His own. I was contacted by a friend of mine who was in the insurance business. He asked if I would be interested in selling insurance on the side. He worked for a fairly large firm, and they had a program that targeted teachers and their families with an insurance program that was an investment opportunity. It started when the kids were young and continued throughout their life for twenty years. You stopped paying in twenty years and then let the interest continue to build for as long as you wanted. It was a good nest egg for school or whatever you wanted to earmark it for. I liked the idea because you didn't have to die to collect your money. As my friend pointed out, I had a captive clientele with all the teachers I knew. I thought what the heck? I took the classes and the insurance test. Low and behold, I became an insurance representative.

The insurance business was very good. As a matter of fact, I was making far more money in the insurance business than I did at teaching school. I would schedule as many appointments right after school as I could. I had five schools to draw from at first. Once one person bought into the program, it was easy to convince a number of others to do the same. Business was so good, we decided to move back to our hometown, and I was going to sell insurance and not teach school. Selling insurance came very easily to me. The big reason was that I believed in the product, and I had bought into the program myself. I was ready to take on the community where I was born.

Chapter Ten

My "Hard Hat" Days

Two weeks prior to our move, I was contacted by a member of my family, and he asked me if I would be interested in going to work in construction. I told him I knew nothing about building. He relayed to me that it was a sales position, and he knew that I was selling insurance. He said that he knew the owner of a company who had a franchise for Butler Buildings, and they were looking for someone to sell the product. *(I didn't know what a Butler Building was.)* My thought on the matter was if I can convince someone to pay me for some intangible, I surely would be able to convince someone to buy something tangible like a building. Two days later, I was in Pittsburgh, Pennsylvania interviewing for the sales job. The very next morning I received an offer of $35,000.00 annual salary, a company car with gas card, and an open expense account. (*Dear Mother*) That was quite exciting, since I was used to making only about $15,000 as a teacher and an insurance representative. One week later, we moved back home and my construction career was underway.

Many people have asked, "How did you make the transition from teaching school to construction management?" My answer was always that the two occupations were very much the same, but in construction, the kids are just bigger. Actually, my early days in construction were in sales, and I spent a lot of my time learning the product that I was selling—Butler Buildings. There were pricing seminars, product understanding seminars,

design-build seminars, etc., all of which were held at beautiful locations—Snowmass, Colorado, Boston, Massachusetts, Orlando, Florida, and places like that. The first one was held in Snowmass, Colorado. When I woke up the first morning, I looked out the curtain on the sliding glass door and there were the Rockies just staring back at me. I looked at my watch and realized I'd be going to my second period class right now, but here I was in the Rocky Mountains. I immediately grabbed my telephone and called the guys I used to work with just to rub it in. The seminars usually lasted three or four days, and the other days of the week were for traveling. So, it was like being on vacation for me. At one time, I spent two weeks in Boston because the marketing department set me up with back-to-back seminars, and I had all weekend to myself. I spent it touring the city of Boston. All I could say to myself was that this was a tough way to make a living. No more nosy kids or lunch and bathroom duty. No, only the good life for me now.

After learning as much as I could about Butler Buildings, which by the way are glorified metal buildings, I started out on the cold call, salesman routine. I began making sales calls on anyone and everyone who would ever want or need a metal building. Everything from two-story office buildings to storage buildings was available at the right price. My job was to not only sell the product, but also as part of the sale, I had to estimate the cost, order the materials, and project manage the construction. As part of the ordering of materials, I had to establish a color for the wall panels and trim that was a part of the building. On one particular large order, which was for a major industry in the town, the owner was adding on to his existing building, and he wanted to match the existing wall panels in style and color. The value of the wall panels was almost $100,000. In preparing my order, I took the product book to the existing building and held the color sample up to the wall panel. I matched the color and finished my order form.

Sometime later, the owner asked me for a sample of the color, and I gave him the sample from my book. When I showed it to him, he told me that the color didn't match his existing building. When I looked at it, it looked like a perfect match. I showed my boss and he agreed with the owner. It wasn't close. He picked out the color, and of course, the owner was happy. I never did tell my boss during my interview that I was color-blind, because I didn't realize that was going to be part of my responsibility. Orders came down from my boss that I was not to pick any colors from that day forward. I had to agree as this would have cost the company $100,000, since the color was considered to be a "special color mix." (*Dear Mother*)

Chapter Eleven

Mom's Last Days

For two years, I worked as the Butler representative and then was given the opportunity to go on site and work as an assistant project manager on one of the largest projects ever built in the state. It was a new replacement medical center with a $90 million price tag. In 1982, that was a lot of money. My office was in one of four trailers located at the site location, and I reported there everyday for two years. I had the chance to learn from one of the best construction management firms in the country. I've used what I learned from them throughout my career. Working at this project afforded me many opportunities. The greatest one was being able to be near my mom as she spent her last fifty-two days of life at the hospital that we were replacing. The old hospital sat on a hill adjacent to the new location. Every morning when

I got to work, I would go up to her room and check on her. Her bed was situated in the room so she could look right out of her window down onto the job site. She would kid me as I would go in to see her before I would head for home at the end of the day.

She would tell me, "I saw you this morning, and you looked like a mother hen and her little chicks. You would be in front of the line with a roll of papers under your arm and following behind you, single file, was a group of men. You were just a-talking and a-talking."

She always told me I was "one-fourth knowledge and three-fourths BS." I never knew when she was peering out of her window and watching me, but I made it a point that whenever I went outside and walked where I could see her window, I would always wave as if she were looking. Most of the time she was.

It was day fifty-two at 2:10 a.m. on October 15, 1985 when I got the call from the hospital. I had asked the doctor to be sure to call me and not my dad. Mom had deteriorated to the point that she really didn't recognize anyone. I always felt that she would smile every time I went to see her and give her my report for the day. The weekend before she died, I went in on a Saturday, and she was not responding well at all. I decided that it was time to prepare. I sat alongside her bed and began to scribe her obituary. I would write a few sentences and then repeat them to get her permission to use the words. She always helped me write my speeches and papers while I was in school, so why should this be any different? That same day I contacted the funeral home where she wanted to be and the church. I made sure everything was taken care of. All that had to be done was to make one call to the funeral director, and he would take care of the rest. The ringing phone brought me out of a deep sleep and I scrambled to find it. Phone calls at that time of the night were not good calls.

"Hello," I said.

The voice on the other end of the line said, "Mr. Glendenning, your mother passed away five minutes ago in her sleep."

I asked if there was anyone with her, and the nurse said that there were two nurses with her changing her bed covers. When they had rolled her on her side, she sighed, and the end finally arrived. I thanked her and told her that I would be right there. Mom had always felt bad when Grandma Sarge passed away because she was alone in the old age home.

She would tell me, "No one should be by themselves when they die."

I got out of bed, walked out on the deck, and looked up into the sky. There was one real bright star standing alone off to the side, and I knew she was looking down on me saying goodbye. I have never cried as hard as I did that night. *(Dear Mother)*

I went to the hospital to see mom for the last time. Funeral homes are not the same. It is a very artificial happening to see your loved one like that. I got to her floor and slowly walked to her room. There were a couple of nurses doing some final touchups. When they saw me, they said they were sorry, and they left the room. Mom was finally at peace. The last fifty-two days were very hard on her. She had been dealing with cancer for over twenty years, and she was finally able to rest. I made the call to the funeral director, and as promised, he took care of the rest.

I had to wait until about 7:00 a.m. before I went to see my dad. He usually slept until 6:30 and then got up to fix his coffee. It was only 3:30 a.m., so I had some time. The only place open was Eat and Park, or what I call "Eat and Puke." I went there and got a coffee, a newspaper, and sat until it was time to go tell dad. He must have seen my car pull up in the driveway, because he met me at the door. He asked me what I was doing up so early.

My response to him was, "It's all over. Mom is finally at peace."

We spent the next five minutes holding on to each other for the first time in our lives. The rest of the week flew by, and it was a good thing. Everything was in order, and my dad couldn't have made any decisions in the state he was in. I'm glad I had the chance to have everything ready for him.

Even though mom was gone, she never really left as far as I was concerned. She and I were always very close, and I could feel the closeness even though she was gone. I would find myself talking to her and asking for her advice on particular matters. Before every theatrical performance (*that's a story in itself*), I would ask her to help me get through the show. After all, she was my biggest fan, and she never let me down.

It was very difficult going back to the site where we were building the medical center. I remember parking at my office trailer and going right inside. I didn't walk up to the old building to visit mom. I would pass by the side of the old building and look up to the room on the corner of the seventh floor where she would sit and watch the mother hen with her chicks in a single file bringing up the rear. For the rest of the project, I kept up her belief in me and utilized her wisdom with my *"one- fourth wisdom and three-fourths BS."(Dear Mother)*

Chapter Twelve

CHANGE IN MANAGEMENT

FIVE MONTHS BEFORE THE PROJECT was to be completed, I was given an opportunity by the company I was working for to go back into the office only as general manager of operations. It seems that the person who hired me five years earlier helped himself to money belonging to the company, and they were going to fire him. I was offered his position. I wanted to complete the project that I was working on, however, this was a long-term opportunity, so I thought, and I agreed to take the job. At the time, there were eight people in the office, and I felt I could get the support from all of them. My ex-boss was fired and he already had his own company in place. I didn't know if any of the existing employees would remain loyal to him and leave with him, but they didn't. I started the transition by doing a makeover of the office. Paint, wallpaper, carpet, and new furniture were the order of the day. My intent was to create a new atmosphere in the office, and it worked. We landed several good jobs, and everyone was pleased with the changes. Then reality struck a sour note.

While I was working at the project site, I was not up to speed with what was going on inside the corporation itself. My world revolved around the medical center and not the home office. When I took over the lead position, I then was made aware of the financial condition we were facing. The main office was located in one state and our office was in another. The work they did was on the corporate books, and our work appeared in the corporate books, but as a separate operation. I realized that the main office was in trouble, and they were counting on our success to keep them afloat. This was not possible. Their overhead was far in excess of our annual volume. All we could do was book as much work as we could to turn a good profit. This lasted for almost a year. Then I was called to a meeting in the main office on a Saturday afternoon. I knew what was happening. The company that had been in business for fifty-five years was going to close. My office had just recently started three jobs, and I was told to complete them but I couldn't go after anymore work. On the following Monday, I called a meeting of our staff and delivered the news. I told them to start looking for other employment opportunities. One month later, the main office closed and laid all of their employees off. I had lost all but two of my staff and had relocated from our refurbished office to a two-room office located over a real estate business. The work I had was coming to a close, and my last act as an employee was to drive a pickup truck with two file cabinets and a desk to the main office. I parked it in the back of the building and locked the keys in the truck. My thirteen years of service to the company had come to an end. (*Dear Mother*)

While I was teaching school, driving a bus, selling insurance, and had started working construction, my brother was also working construction. He, however, went to work with a very large firm and stayed with them for over twenty years. He was also involved with some of the largest construction in the state. One particular job found him doing a state job for two years that ended up in court. The company he worked for and the state were at odds with the final costs of a particular project. For a year after the project was completed, he was involved in the court proceedings. It burned him out as far as large construction was concerned. He left the big company after beating the state in court and went to work for a very small remolding contractor who was located in our hometown. I had talked with him a couple of times, and he informed me that his boss wanted to hire someone to sell metal buildings for him. I thought about the possibility and decided to interview for the job. I met with his boss and was hired that day. The business was run out of an old house and my office was set up on the sun porch. It wasn't the best of conditions but there was nothing else around. My brother and I went out for lunch, and we talked about the possibility of him and me going into business for ourselves. Why work for someone else and let them reap the profits of our toils? Besides that, our boss was a real jerk. So, we finally made the decision and laid the groundwork for starting our own company. The day finally came and we both turned in our notice at the same time. That's when the Brothers Corporation was founded. We wrote our business plan, went to the bank, and borrowed the money to get us underway. We both owned property and had to use it as collateral for the loan. After all the "T's" were crossed and the "I's" dotted, we were finally in business. Brothers Corporation was ready to make its mark in the construction world.

For six years, we continued to do business in our hometown. We wanted to build our reputation within the community, and we did the things necessary to maintain it. Chamber of Commerce, Rotary, Big Brothers and Sisters, etc., were the order of the times. We made sure that we attended all the necessary public assemblies that would count. The biggest accomplishment that we made was being selected as the construction manager for a $3.5 million Catholic church. That project really put us on the map and it happened just one month from the time we had opened our doors. For five-and-one-half years, we maintained the business and all seemed to be going well. Then it seemed as if the business climate went dry. We couldn't buy a job. The profit margins were dropping and dropping. At one point, we had eleven carpenters working for us, and we finally had to lay most of them off. Work in the area slowed to nothing but the bills kept showing up. We finally had to shut the business down six years after we opened our doors. As happy as we were when we opened up, it was a very sad day when we locked the doors for the last time. My brother and I drove off in different directions out of the parking lot that day, and we have never crossed paths except when our dad passed away five years later. *(Dear Mother)*

Chapter Thirteen

DAD

MY DAD, LIKE SO MANY other men who lost their wives, became a total recluse. We tried to get him involved in outside activities, but all he wanted to do was sit in his recliner and watch the weather channel. He even moved out of the bedroom that he had shared with my mom because of old memories. My sister was living with him, along with her three children, so there was always activity going on. Still, he remained cloistered within himself until one day one of his granddaughter's friends came to visit with her dad. His name was Bill, and he and my dad hit it off from the very beginning. They had common interests between them, and they knew a lot of the same people. Bill would come by, get my dad, and they would just go for rides. Dad even went so far as to buy a new car. He always enjoyed buying cars because he would give the salesmen such a hard time. His knowledge of the car parts would allow him to ask the type of questions that most salesmen couldn't begin to answer. Most of the time the questions didn't have anything to do with his purchase of the car, but he loved it when the salesmen would say, "Boy, you sure know your cars." Dad's eyes were getting so bad that he would have Bill take him around. Strangely enough, my dad loved to target shoot at the gun range. When he was much younger, he was on the local shooting team and would compete with other towns at the range. The diabetes had its way with his eyes, and he had a hard time reading and doing the close things. However, put him on a target range with his .22 target rifle in hand, and he would shoot very well. Bill also liked to shoot or at least that's what he told my dad. He would be amazed at my dad's shooting accuracy. I witnessed his shooting prowess on many occasions and was also amazed how well he would do.

The other activity that my dad enjoyed was fishing. Growing up, my dad and I would go catfishing whenever he had the time. We enjoyed sitting on the river bank, leaning back against a rock with the carbide light glowing, and casting enough light for us to see our lines in the water. One afternoon I left work early and picked up my dad. I took him to the river. I had packed all the fishing gear and bait and had worked out a deal with a friend of mine to use his boat. We fished until midnight, and we only caught three catfish—three catfish in seven hours. Some people would call that crazy, but I have the memory of that evening laughing and seeing my dad really enjoying himself, that I will never forget.

Dad had been giving himself insulin shots for over forty years. After mom died, he announced that he was finished taking insulin, and if he died because of it, that's just the way it goes. My sister moved out of state with her husband and took my dad with her. I think that when he left the house, it was both good and bad. Getting him out of the house and into a new environment helped him through those years of getting used to not having mom around. However, not being in the house meant that he had to leave a lot of memories behind. I could tell that he was slowly wearing down. My sister got him to go to a doctor who put him on some oral medication instead of the shots for the diabetes. However, the doctor said that his body was wearing out, and there was really nothing that could be done. I got a call from my sister one day while I was at work, and she said that dad had a stroke, was in the hospital, and I had better get there. I made the normal eight-hour trip in a little over six hours. I sat with him for two days while he was in the hospital. He rallied and was discharged to a special care facility so he could be watched around the clock. The second call from my sister came two weeks later. She told me that he had passed away during the night. Sitting with my dad in the hospital after the first call, I had held his hand all night long and talked to him about how he was going to be fine. When I left the next morning, which was the last time I saw him alive, I bent over and kissed him on the forehead. I told him to say hi to mom for me and to tell her that I loved her. *(Dear Mother)*

Chapter Fourteen

SHRINERS HOSPITAL
FOR CHILDREN

ONE OF THE HIGHLIGHTS OF my career was the two years I spent in Philadelphia working on the construction management team for the Shriners Hospital for Children. During the time we spent working on the project, I had the chance to meet and interact with not only the doctors and nurses, but even more exciting was that I got to interact with the kids who made the hospital their home during their recovery times. One particular young girl, who had lost the feeling in her arms and hands as a result of a car wreck on her prom night, really caught my heart and she became my "special friend."

I had to go to the old hospital a couple days a week for meetings and to get information concerning programming needs during the building of the new facility. The old hospital was about sixty-five years old. Although it was very clean, it was really starting to look its age. One day I had gone to the old facility and I was walking down the hall. The kids were all over the place. The staff made sure that these kids really stayed busy, and every activity had some kind of therapy involved. As I passed this one room, I noticed a young, very thin girl sitting at the work table in her room. She was trying to stack blocks on top of each other.

I stepped inside the room and said, "Would you like to have a job helping me build the new hospital?"

As she turned around, all I could see was this fresh young face with a big smile. She wore a ball cap that said Alabama on the front of it.

"I sure will," came this deep southern drawl back at me.

I asked her if she was from Alabama and she said that she was. I told her I never would have guessed. I told her that she talked funny, and she said that she didn't think that she did, but she thought that I did.

From that very moment, this young southern belle and I became friends. I made it a point that whenever I was at the old facility, I would check in on Ellie. It seems that she was a senior in high school, and on the night of her prom, she and her date were hit by a drunk driver. That's what caused her injuries. She was a paraplegic who was receiving new innovative electrode implants that would stimulate the nerves in her arms and hands so she could once again use them. She had been at Shriners for about two months and would be there after the surgery for a year. She was really excited about being one of the first to move into the new facility. I nicknamed her "Alabama" and I told her that name would stick with her for the rest of her life. Unlike most of the children there, her family was not staying at the facility, and she only got to see her mom about every two weeks. Her dad was not around. So, I think that I filled in during some of those lonely periods, and it was good for both of us.

We planned to have some of the kids come over to the new facility during construction and have pizza with the workers. We set up tables and made sure that the kids were mingled in with the workers while they ate. Most of the kids were in wheelchairs, and it didn't take long for the workers to pair off with the kids. We had tours all over the building. I made sure that "Alabama" was part of the group that I took around. I always liked working with the older kids. They housed the kids by age groups so all of the one's in my group would be staying together in the same unit when we opened the doors. Even though there was no paint on the walls or ceilings, no furniture or floor covering, the kids really liked their new home.

My little southern friend had her operation and at first struggled with the equipment. But, not long after the surgery, she could hold some items, but she still couldn't do much with them. Her therapist said that would come later. I tried to always bring her something to keep her spirits up when I visited her, and the one thing that made her smile the most was a pink hard hat with Alabama written across the front.

Twenty months from when we started, we were ready to open the doors to the new facility. All the kids were transported in ambulances with two army helicopters overhead leading the group down Broad Street. We were followed by the Shrine's marching band, clowns, little cars, motorcycles, and a complete police escort. The entire staff from both the Shrine Hospital and Temple University formed a pathway into the facility and through the lobby to the elevators. As the kids were wheeled in their chairs or beds, the entire crowd applauded with such enthusiasm you could hardly hear the band. Police sirens sounded their salute, and as I looked around at the people in attendance, I couldn't see a dry eye anywhere. I saw "Alabama" being wheeled by her mom up the human pathway, and I became as everyone else with the tears rolling down my face and a smile from ear to ear. (*Dear Mother*)

Chapter Fifteen

THE THEATRE

I HAVE ALWAYS ENJOYED THE theatre. It didn't make any difference what I did. It was the simple fact that I enjoyed being in any part of it. To be truthful, I think I enjoyed performing on stage more than anything else. My first performance as an actor took place while I was in kindergarten. It was during a Christmas play, and I was asked to play the donkey that Mary rode into Bethlehem. I never thought of it at that time, but the main reason that I got the part was that I had the stature to have some girl ride on my back while I crawled around on all fours. I had the donkey costume and all. Little did I know that that was only the beginning of my theatrical career. I performed in the normal school plays, however, it wasn't until college when I joined the community theatre group. That's when I really got into the performance part of the arts.

I enjoyed acting and singing in the musicals. Although I performed in a couple of dramatic performances, I really enjoyed musical comedies the best. The audiences were much easier to play to, and it was just more enjoyable. The Inquisition, Camelot, Walk Down Memory Lane, Oklahoma, A Few Good Men, Wait Until Dark, Annie, (I did this show twice) Little Mary Sunshine, Filzaria, The Pink Panther Stalks Again, Lend Me A Tenor, The Lion In Winter and Music Man, to name a few, were the shows that I had the chance to be in. I loved performing on stage especially in the musicals. During my undergraduate years, I was a physical education major with a speech and English minor. I was expected to perform in the shows that were presented by the drama department. This then carried into my teaching career and followed me into my construction days. There is something relaxing about good community theatre. My favorite show was Annie because I got to interact with the kids. It was extremely important to bond with them and then it was more believable on stage. I was lucky to have been paired with a tremendously talented group. It really made my job much easier and enjoyable.

When it became next to impossible to work in a show, I would always try to locate a theater wherever I was and go see some shows just to keep the grease paint running through my veins. I was fortunate to be assigned projects in some larger cities where you can find both good and bad theatre. Detroit, Baltimore, Richmond, etc., all had excellent theatre, and I tried to take advantage of it. I even attended a gay theatre in Philadelphia one evening, and to say the least, it was an experience. The set was arranged in the round, which meant that it was a complete circle and the audience sat around it. Of the one-hundred seats, there wasn't a bad one in the house. The theatre was on the second floor of a building in the theatre district, and to get to it you had to ride an old freight elevator (the kind with the two doors that went up and down). The only way we found our way into the theatre was that we followed a small group of people to the right door to get in. As we all piled into the elevator, I noticed that one of the guys had a nose piercing with a chain that led from his nose to his lip and then to his wallet that was in his back pocket. Multi-colored hair was the attire for the evening. When we arrived at the second floor, it was obvious that we were the oddballs of this group. We sat on the top row with our backs to the wall so we could see everything both on and off the stage. The performance was pretty good with a lot of homosexual activities throughout the show. However, they were performed very low key, and it wasn't uncomfortable to watch. As soon as the show was over, we didn't waste any time getting out of the building and back to the car. I looked at the evening as an educational experience and not as an entertainment venue. It was a far cry from my days of crawling around with a donkey costume on and having little Anne Michael ride on my back. (*Dear Mother*)

Chapter Sixteen

MY "OTHER" LOVE

DURING THOSE EARLY CAREER YEARS, I kept very busy. It seemed as if there was something going on every night. From 1968 to 1985, I officiated basketball on three levels. These included high school, junior college, and NCAA Division I. For seventeen years, I worked up the ranks in basketball, and officiated until my final year, when I blew out my knee during a college game. I never blew the whistle again,

That year I had sixty-five ballgames scheduled. However, in January of 1985, during a game in West Virginia, I injured my knee so badly that I had to officiate the game standing on the half-court line, and my partner worked both end lines. That poor man had to run from one end to the other, and the final score of the game was 115 to 112. That was a hard week for me because I had to give the commissioner the rest of my basketball schedule. That's when I went under the knife for a major knee repair. (This was the third one I had.) I really enjoyed blowing the whistle, and to me, the tighter the game, the more I enjoyed it. Many of my colleagues would get uptight before a big game and their nerves would get the best of them. To me, it was like being back on stage. When working up through the ranks, you had to prove your abilities to the commissioner who, after he was satisfied that you could handle yourself on the court, would then move you up to the higher level of play. So, I had my "baptism by fire" by working everything from pee wee ball to what I called the "toothless wonders," which were the over thirty-five men's league on Saturday night during my training period. If you could work these games and keep everyone from getting hurt, you were doing a good job according to the commissioner. That group of overweight men, at some point in their basketball careers, was no doubt decent ballplayers. However, now it was all they could do to keep from having a heart attack while running up and down the court. In an effort to control the possibility of injury, we would make sure that the clock ran constantly, even during foul shots. This would allow the game to be much shorter. We would also allow eight time-outs instead of the regular five. That provided them with more rest periods. Don't get me wrong. That league of "has been's" was not completely without talent. There were a couple of teams that had some definite "ringers" on their roster, and they could really play the game way above the rim. One particular team came from the inner city of Baltimore, and their name was the "Midnight Cats." Those boys could play ball with any college team in the area, and they dominated the league with their dunks, blocks, and ball-handling ability. Their center was six-foot-nine and their point guard was six-foot-three. They had the largest following of fans in the league. When they were doing their warm-ups, the fans would circle around the court and cheer their team on. Their coach's name was "Shocky." I could never figure out what it meant, but he certainly was in charge of the team. He kept them under control, and he was always trying to intimidate the refs. He would shout at every call you made if it was against his team, and he would run up and down the sidelines coaching his team and yelling at the refs. During one particular game, Shocky was his normal vocal self, and I had a real close charging call on one of his men under the basket. The man on his team came charging into the basket, and he let the ball fly toward the basket. Wouldn't you know, it went in. However, when he released the ball, he charged into the defensive forward and down he went. I came charging out from under the basket signaling no basket and the foul was on the Midnight Cats. There I was, the only white guy in a five-mile radius, and I had just called an offensive foul on the best player of the Cats and took away his basket. When I turned around, I was standing toe-to-toe with Shocky. Now, he was not an intimidating figure. He was all of about five-foot-seven with a little round belly. He was screaming at the top of his lungs right into my face.

Then I very calmly looked into his eyes and said, "Coach, it's going to cost you one technical foul for every step it takes you to get back to your bench."(He didn't realize that he was standing in the foul circle out on the court.) Shocky, without missing a beat, puckered his lips and whistled toward his bench. He waved his hand and instructed his men to pick him up and carry him back to the bench. No technical fouls were called that night. The Cats won by thirty-five points, and I made a friend for life named "Coach Shocky."

I discovered early in my refereeing career that it didn't help your chances of survival in the various basketball leagues if you presented an attitude that you were never wrong. I never raised my voice if I was chastising a player or coach, and I never let my true emotions show. If it got down to having to throw a player or coach out of the game, I did it with very little flair. You see, that's what they wanted. They wanted the referee to get tied up in the call and take his mind off of the matter at hand. I once officiated a game where a fight broke out between two players in the top of the key. It escalated very quickly into a bench-clearing brawl, and I knew that I wasn't going to be able to stop it with my whistle. I quickly jumped on top of the scoring table, and began marking down numbers of those players throwing punches or causing the melee to continue. I let the school administration and the coaches control their teams. When the fighting ended, I had both teams go to their locker rooms, and I met the coaches at the scorer's table. The home coach was very upset because he had brought his mother to the game, and she was sitting in the first row behind her son's bench. It was a good seat for the game but not the fight. She ended up getting punched in the side of the head by a fan who was aiming for her son, the coach. (*Dear Mother*) When I had both coaches' attention, I pulled out my notebook and announced to the home coach that six of his team were out of the game and the visitors would be shooting twelve technical fouls. The smile on the visiting coach's face was a Norman Rockwell moment. It only lasted for a second, because I had to inform him that he would be losing seven men and the home team would be shooting fourteen technical foul shots. They would be given the ball out of bounds. So, for the next ten minutes, we shot foul shots—first on one end of the court and then on the other. Both teams only had five players left on their teams, and the rest of the game went without incident. I received a letter from the Supervisor of Officials later that week, and when I saw the envelope, I thought this doesn't look good. However, the Commissioner of Officials was at the ballgame that night and had observed the entire situation. He felt that I handled the situation in the best manner that could have happened. I really felt good after I read the letter, and felt with that under my belt, I was ready for anything.

You would think that officiating college basketball would eliminate some of the weird things that had happened when coming up through the ranks. However, as I found out, college ball was no different. Like the time I was working a Division 1 game on the East coast. I was working the end line under the basket in a rather small facility. The cheering squad was also on the end line about a step back from the paint. As the ball was being tossed back and forth, it found its way to the other side of the court. I then took my position halfway across the end line. At the same time, the cheerleaders started their chant, which also included a kick line routine. As the kick line started, the ball came across the court. As I started to back up, I was immediately kicked in the butt by two enthusiastic cheerleaders. I don't know who was the most embarrassed—the cheerleaders or me. Needless to say, the crowd loved it.

ॐ ॐ ॐ

I WAS WORKING A GAME in Pittsburg, Pennsylvania, and was standing at center court with my partner prior to the game starting. Both teams were warming up and the game was on TV. I noticed the floor man for the TV production crew coming towards us, and I thought he was going to discuss the time-out process which is different when the game is televised.

However, to my surprise, the floor man came up to me and said, "Excuse me, ref, but would you mind putting some powder on your head, because the lights are casting quite a reflection back to the cameras."

The look on my face must have been something to behold, because he said, "Just joking; have a good game."

As I was working up through the ranks, I would hear someone in the stands yell, "Come on, SPOT, get in the game."

The more years I worked, the remark turned into, "Come on, BALDY, get into the game."

I didn't have a chance and Rogaine had not been invented yet.

A referee doesn't often have a chance to get even with someone in the crowd who is quite loud and does everything under the sun to get a rise out of you. As a good official knows, the last thing you need is to have "rabbit ears." This is when a referee hears everything that is said to him by the crowd and lets it affect his calls. This was not the case with me. I didn't let the noise in the crowd bother me except this one time. I was working a Division 1 college game at a Catholic school in northern Pennsylvania. The visitors were out of New York, and they were having their way with the local college Catholic team. During the course of the game, there was a gentleman who had a large drum. He was using it to get his message across that he was not happy with the way the game was going, and it was my fault. Every time I made a call against the local school, he would "sound off" on the drum with a chant that was directed to me.

"Get the ref a toupee. Get the ref a toupee," and so on. Over and over he would pound the drum and shout at the top of his lungs. I now believe there is justice in this world because during the second half of the ballgame, with his team behind by thirty-five points, he decided he needed to go to the concession stand. I could only imagine that his throat must have been dry with all of that chanting. I really hadn't paid any attention to him leaving, but I really noticed him on his way back to the stands. I was working the sideline when all of a sudden there was an intercepted pass and a quick fast break was underway. I made a turn as the ball passed me and was being driven down the court in a very speedy fast break. As I continued to watch the players and made an effort to get in front of the fast break, out of the corner of my eye I saw the "Little Drummer Boy" coming up the side line with a giant Coke in one hand and an extra large bag of popcorn in the other. Now, I don't want to give you the wrong impression when I said the "Little Drummer Boy." He was actually about five-foot-ten, and weighed about 200 pounds. He was talking to the crowd as the play was happening. I caught a glimpse of him and I had already shifted gears. I headed at full force in an effort to catch up with the play when I lowered my shoulder just enough to catch him on his right side. When we met, I never lost stride and continued to follow the play to the end line. As I turned to square up with the court, I glanced back in the direction I had come from, and caught sight of justice in action. Two rows of spectators about four people wide were standing and wiping off their faces and clothes. In the center of the two rows, I could see two shoes upside down and pointed toward the ceiling attached to two legs, and that was all. The rest of the "Little Drummer Boy's" body was buried in the bleachers. I really felt bad for the innocent bystanders, but I'm sure that sometime during the course of the game they had screamed some obscenity at me. It was a matter of being in the wrong place at the wrong time. The visiting team made their basket and we started up the court again. This time I saw the "Little Drummer Boy" standing soaked with Coke, and popcorn dotted his hair. On the outside world, all that was visible was my referee face, but on the inside, I had the biggest smile in the world. Did I get even that night? Oh, yes, I certainly did. *(Dear Mother)*

What makes a person want to be an official of any type? Why would anyone want to subject themselves to the harassment that seems to go along with the job? There is something about having the power to stop the action of an exciting contest, make a ruling that only you saw clearly, and then sell it to the coaches, teams, and the fans. Sports officials are only one-half right or wrong, depending on which side of the field or court you are standing on.

Take for instance the time I was asked to work a high school game in the southern part of West Virginia. When I was called the athletic director of the school, I questioned why I was asked to work the game. At that time, I was working in the West Virginia College Conference and had not worked a high school game for two years, only the state tournaments. So, when I was contacted for the game, I asked the question, "WHY?" The athletic director explained that the game was a very big game for the area, and they didn't want any local people involved with it. The two teams were bitter rivals, and the two coaches were known to have given referees a real hard time working the games in the past. The site for the game was a school in the southern part of West Virginia, which also happened to be the home of Willy Akers, a former player at West Virginia University and coach of the favorite team. The hometown fans loved Willy, and he could do no wrong. He liked to intimidate the referees to the point that he could control the game entirely if the referee would let him. However, I never worked any of his games, and as far as I was concerned, it was just another game. I had accepted this high school game for Friday night and had to drive into Charleston to work a college game on Saturday night. Then I planned to head home on Sunday. The gymnasium was not a very large building and it held around 800 fans. That night it was holding about 2,000 fans because the team that won would be going to the state tournament. Everyone just knew that Willy would be going to the "Big Dance." There were so many spectators that the court was oblong due to the fact there were so many people standing on the sidelines and end lines to watch. I asked the athletic director to move the crowd back as far as possible so they wouldn't interfere with the game. If there was ever a home team advantage, it certainly was in the house that night. Their only problem was that the visiting team came to play, and play they did. They were not intimidated by the fans, the home team, or Willy himself. They were there to play and win. And that is exactly what happened. The game was extremely fast for a high school game, and by halftime, the visiting team was ahead by twenty-five points. Willie's kids were not in the same league that night. To top everything off, the two referees were cheaters, blind, and knew nothing about the game of basketball. At halftime, the athletic director had hired two policemen to escort us back to our locker room because it was obvious there were some fans who wanted a piece of us. The second half was an exact copy of the first half. By the end of the game, the final score was ninety-five to fifty in favor of the visiting team. We were not only escorted back to our locker room, but the police stayed around, walked us to our cars, and led us out of town. That was the first time I was ever escorted out of town after a game; a high school game at that. *(Dear Mother)*

Have you ever had a day when you just knew that something was going to happen? It's just a feeling and you're not sure where it is, but it's there anyhow. I worked basketball with many different partners. Sometimes, my partner would live close so we could ride to the game together, and it was good having someone else with you especially on the ride home. Basketball is a winter sport and many a night in January and February the snow would be flying, and we would be driving down the road heading home talking about the game. This one night I worked a game that was about four hours away from my house. I worked with a man who lived about an hour away, so I said that I would pick him up on the way to the game and drop him off on my way home. I always wore a white shirt and tie to the games, and I carried my black and whites in my athletic bag. That way I could shower after the game and feel comfortable on the drive home. Besides, I felt that was the professional way to go to and from the game. My partner, on the other hand, felt the need for speed as he would wear his black and whites to the game, and after the game, he would not shower. Instead, he would put on his overcoat over the top of his sweaty uniform and drive home all bundled up. He would keep his coat at the scorer's table, so at the end of the game, he could just grab it and then out the door he would go. On this one particular night, we were on our way to the school and my partner seemed quite uncomfortable for some reason. I asked him what was bothering him. He said that his stomach was upset, and he didn't feel good. Traveling north to the gym was bad enough, but this night it was really bad outside. The snow was blowing fiercely and it was sticking to the windshield, which made it very hard to see. I was concentrating on where the road was and wasn't paying attention to my shotgun rider.

All of a sudden he yelled, "STOP THE CAR NOW!"

Of course, I slammed on the brakes, and we proceeded to slide across the road, spun around, and came back across the road to the correct side but only in about a foot of snow.

"What the hell is the matter with you?" I bellowed.

My partner screamed back at me, "I have to take a dump right now" and out the passenger door he bounced.

Now, you have to visualize this. It's twenty-five degrees outside, and the snow is coming down at about six inches per hour. The wind is blowing at forty miles per hour, and my partner is heading out into this field, lifting up his overcoat, undoing his pants, and his underwear is dragging in the snow at his ankles. Then he squats like a cub bear in the wilds. I could barely make him out but he was there with his overcoat pulled over his head. I could tell he was slowly feeling better. I settled back into my warm seat and waited for his return. The passenger door opened. There he stood with the coat still on his head and his pants around his knees covered with snow. Then he posed the million dollar question of the night.

"DO YOU HAVE ANY TOILET PAPER?"

My reply to him was, "No, but I have <u>five ones for a five</u>."

He never spoke to me the rest of the night, and I didn't ask him what he used for toilet paper that evening. I can only imagine that somewhere on that road there is a very fertile spot in the field where plants seem to grow better than anywhere else, and I know why! *(Dear Mother)*

Chapter Seventeen

WHAT IT ALL MEANS

WHEN I LOOK OVER MY shoulder and gaze at my life, I have to laugh at some of the things that have happened to me—like all of the things in this book. All of the stories that I have reported are true, and I have only changed the names of the people out of respect for them. As far-fetched as some of them sound, I can attest that they did happen, and they did happen to me. I can remember my mom telling me during the summer when I was a kid, and I was complaining how slowly the time was going that summer, she said one day I wouldn't be able to keep up with the time. Things will seem to pass you by without stopping, and if you blink your eyes, you will miss it. How right she was. It seems that today I find it next to impossible to keep up sometimes. My children have grown into adults, and I have four grandchildren who now keep them going. I can't even imagine trying to keep up with their schedules. I have always lived and worked on the East Coast and was able to keep in contact with the kids. We were never more than six hours apart. It was fairly easy to pick up one day and head to the mountains for the weekend in an effort to spend time with them. We always tried to catch some of the ballgames and tried to be as much a part of their lives as possible. Then, my wife and I decided to move to the Midwest so that we could be closer to her parents who were getting up there in years and obviously needed help from time to time. Although my wife came from a family of five, she seemed to have the instincts required to help those who were always there for her. We now live about forty-five minutes from her parents, and we make it a point to help them whenever necessary. That's the way it should be. The only drawback is now my wife and I spend a lot more time sitting on the couch trying to keep awake more than we did before. We also spend our time trying to figure out how and when we can plan a trip to see the kids, because we now have to fly to see them. But, that doesn't stop us, because as Sister Mary Phillip, my seventh grade teacher used to say, "Where there is a will, there is a way." Every parent is proud of their kids and I am no exception. I can truthfully say that the proudest days of my life were when my kids came into this world. My first daughter was born when I was teaching school. I can remember that day as if it were yesterday.

I was teaching English class when over the intercom came a message, "Mr. G., please report to the office immediately."

I knew exactly what was happening because my wife didn't feel well when I had left for work in the morning. I ran down the halls of the school and had a couple of kids scold me for running in the halls, but I didn't care.

When I reached the office, the secretary said, "Your brother-in-law called, and he's taking your wife to the hospital. I was about twenty miles from the hospital, but I think I made it in about ten minutes. As a matter of fact, I pulled up in the driveway right behind my brother-in-law's car with my wife aboard. I got her a wheelchair and sped her into the hospital to the registration desk. They took her right into the labor room and sent me back to the father's waiting room. You see, in those days, fathers were not allowed in the labor and delivery rooms.

I no sooner sat down in this overstuffed chair when the door opened and a nurse announced, "Mr. Glendenning, you have a new baby daughter."

Total time was about ten minutes from when we entered the hospital to the time she was born. That little gift from God has grown up to become a mother of her own with a great husband and two kids that make their grandpa very proud.

Our second daughter came with not as much flair as her sister. We were more ready for her and ended up spending about an hour in the hospital prior to her arrival. She still lives in our hometown with her hardworking husband and our third grandchild. But who is counting? It made it interesting having two in diapers at the same time. Trying to keep them on the same schedule was a job in itself. My wife did a great job, because as I indicated earlier, I wasn't home that much. Keeping the three jobs going kept me busy. We did have family time every once in awhile. There was no doubt that they were daddy's little girls.

Our third child was a special Christmas gift. Yes, you can say that planning wasn't very good to have a baby around Christmas. However, it was time for a boy, and it just so happened that he arrived on Christmas Eve. Needless to say, there weren't many expectant parents in the hospital on Christmas Eve. As a matter of fact, we were the only ones there that evening. This time it took a little while for Santa to find the right building, but he did, and we were presented with this little Christmas gift in a bright red stocking with a little red Santa cap—our third child, our son. It was a joyous time of the year and the two girls, who were just babies themselves, loved their little brother. We had a houseful due to the holidays and the new baby. I think we finally got to sleep about three days later. My son is now married and has made us very proud, both as a great father and an outstanding teacher. He married his high school sweetheart, and they have blessed us with our fourth grandchild.

ఏ ఏ ఏ

MY KIDS HAVE BEEN MY life. Even though there were rocky roads during our marriage, I still maintained my relationship with them. As a result, there has always been a strong bond between me and the kids. It's this bond that kept us together even during the hard times. There is no stronger love than that of a parent for his children.

ટ્ર   ટ્ર   ટ્ર

EVEN THOUGH I DON'T MOVE as quickly as I used to, and I don't remember things as easily as before, as long as my feet hit the floor in the morning, and when I look in the paper and I don't see my name listed on those certain pages, I will continue to have a great time. I will always be that baldheaded referee, clown-faced bus driver, and hard hat toting construction man with lots of stories to tell. This is only the beginning.

(Dear Mother)

EPILOGUE

DEAR MOTHER IS A GATHERING of the lighter side of my life while growing up and trying to make a living. There are many people who are represented in this book, and I would like to thank all of them, for without them, this undertaking would have been impossible. To me, the "stars" of the book are my mom, dad, and my kids. Everything that I did was centered on them, and I would like to thank them for allowing me to relate some of our "special times" to my readers. Special thanks go to my wife, "GG," who was the one who pushed me to make up my mind to write the book. Although she came along later in my life, she has had the greatest influence on me, and I owe the world to her. To all others in the book who are co-stars, I tip my hat to you. If I didn't know you or run into you, I never would have been able to tell everyone about you and what we did. I also would like to thank all the nuns and priests that I have come in contact with and who helped my parents form my ideals about the ways of the world. It was only by their continual efforts that I was able to survive my formative years, convert them into who I am today, and the way I feel. I use my seventh grade teacher's saying, "Where there is a will, there is a way" very often. This philosophy has been part of me for many years, and I have used it very successfully many times.

It provided me with the strength to do things that even surprised me sometimes. As you get older, you find yourself trying to find ways to make yourself keep going no matter what is put in front of you. That saying has allowed me to surpass obstacles that I had to deal with many times. Therefore, it is my gift to you to use it whenever you need it. Remember, laughter is a great medication, and although it may be tough at times to laugh, at least let a little smile show on your face, because your smile could be the best medicine for those you are looking at.

My final philosophy to you is, "Let a Smile Be Your Umbrella and Your Ass Will Get Soaking Wet."

EKIM